TOYS

Contents

G000161532

This is me. I am six. My favourite toy is a Micro Scooter. I like to go fast on it.

This is me today.

More toys from today

Bob the Builder

Plastic Dinosaur

Hogwarts Castle

This is my brother. When he was six, his favourite toy was a Game Boy. He liked to play games on it with his friends.

My brother in 1994.

More toys from the 1990s

Playstation

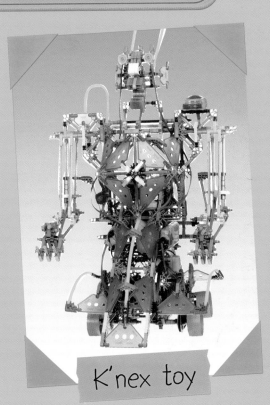

K'nex toy

Spice Girls dolls

This is my sister. When she was five, her favourite toy was a tea set. She liked to have tea parties.

My sister in 1988.

More toys from the 1980s

Remote-controlled robot

Rubik's Cube

Sylvanian Families

This is my mum. When she was seven, her favourite toy was a Spacehopper. She liked to bounce in the air.

My mum in 1971.

More toys from the 1970s

Paddington Bear

Etch A Sketch

Spirograph

This is my dad. When he was six, his favourite toy was a race track. He liked to race cars.

My dad in 1969.

More toys from the 1960s

Sindy dolls

Slinky

Thunderbirds rocket

This is my grandfather. When he was six, his favourite toy was Meccano. He liked to make things.

My grandfather in 1951.

More toys from the 1950s

Teddy bear

Monopoly board game

Toy truck

Toy timeline

Meccano

Race track

Spacehopper

| 1950s | 1960s | 1970s |

Tea set

Game Boy

Micro Scooter

| 1980s | 1990s | 2000s |

Index

16